Parasites & Partners

KILLERS

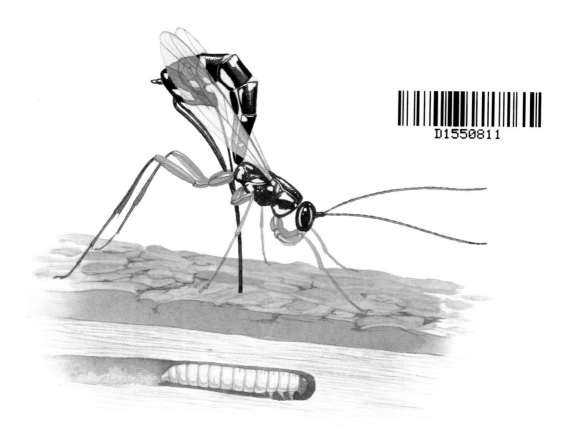

James W. R. Martin

Chicago, Illinois

Chicago, Illinois

First published 2003 by Raintree, a division of Reed Elsevier Inc.
© 2003 The Brown Reference Group plc

Library of Congress Cataloging-in-Publication Data

Martin, James W. R.
  Killers / James W.R. Martin.
    p. cm. — (Parasites and partners)
Summary: A comprehensive look at different types of creatures that kill
or severely damage their hosts, including bacteria that cause diseases,
blood-sucking mosquitoes, and killer insects called parasitoids.
Includes bibliographical references and index.
Microkillers — Controlling body and mind — The weird world of parasitoids.
  ISBN 0-7398-6990-6 (lib. bdg. : hardcover) — ISBN 1-4109-0357-5 (pbk.)
  1. Parasitoids—Juvenile literature. [1. Parasites. 2. Animals—Habits
and behavior.] I. Title. II. Series.
  QL496.12.M37 2003
  577.8'57—dc21

                    2003007051

ISBN 1-4109-0357-5

Printed and bound in Singapore.
1 2 3 4 5 6 7 8 9 0 07 06 05 04 03 02

Acknowledgements

The publisher would like to thank the following for permission to use photographs:

Key: l – left, r – right, c – center, t – top, b – bottom.
Art explosion: 28t; **Bruce Coleman Collection:** Kim Taylor 7, 29; **Cereal Research Center/AAFC:** 5t; **Corbis:** Anthony
Bannister/Gallo Images 24t, Bettman 9b, Michael & Patricia Fogden 20t, George McCarthy 8b, Tony Wharton/FPLA 30;
Image Bank: Per-Eric Berglund 28b; **NHPA:** Anthony Bannister 20b, G. I. Bernard 15, N. A. Callow 18t, E. A. Janes 25;
Oxford Scientific Films: 16, 23, 26, P. J. DeVries 18b; **PHIL:** 5 (background), CDC/Janice Carr 4ct, CDC/PHPP/DMTS/James Gathany
10t; **Science Photo Library:** Jurgen Berger/Max-Planck Institute 12, Eye of Science 27t, David Scharf 9t; **Still Pictures:** Manfred
Kage 13, Jorgen Schytte 10–11; **Stone:** 8t; **USDA/ARS:** 4cb, 5b, Scott Bauer 17, 18–19, 27b, Jack Dykinga 4t, Sanford Porter 21;
Front Cover: NHPA: G. I. Bernard (t); **USDA/ARS:** Scott Bauer (b).

For The Brown Reference Group plc

Project Editor: Jim Martin
Consultancy Board: Dr. Robert S. Anderson,
    Royal Canadian Museum of Nature, Ottawa, Canada;
    Prof. Marilyn Scott, Institute of Parasitology,
    McGill University, Montreal, Canada
Designed by: Pewter Design Associates
Illustrator: Mike Woods
Picture Researcher: Helen Simm
Managing Editor: Bridget Giles
Art Director: Dave Goodman
Production Director: Alastair Gourlay

For Raintree

Editor: Jim Schneider
Managing Editor: Jamie West
Production Manager: Brian Suderski

Front cover: Wasp cocoons on the body of a caterpillar (*top*);
a tsetse fly rests on a flower (*bottom*).

Title page: A parasitic wasp drills through wood to reach
a beetle larva with its egg tube.

Note to the Reader
Some words are shown in bold, like **this.** You can find out what they mean by looking in "Words to Know."

Parasites & Partners
KILLERS

Contents

Introduction

Animals and plants do not live alone. They are always interacting with other creatures. A close association between different species is called a **symbiosis.** *Parasites & Partners* introduces you to symbiotic relationships. You can see examples of these around you every day. Anyone who keeps a dog shares a symbiosis with their pet. The dog is fed and housed by its owner, who gains a companion and protection in return. Both partners in this relationship benefit, but that is not always the case. The different types of symbioses covered in this book are discussed in the box below.

Each book in *Parasites & Partners* looks at a different group of relationships. Find out how plants and animals interact with other types of creatures as they feed, breed, keep clean, find a home, and move around.

Some important words for you to remember

Symbiosis
A relationship between two different types of creatures is called a symbiosis. This bee is taking nectar from the flower to feed its young, while the plant is using the bee to spread its pollen. Both partners benefit in this example.

Parasite
A creature that benefits at the expense of another but does not usually kill it is called a **parasite.** The parasite gains food and, generally, a place to live. This flea is a rat parasite. It lives on the body of a rat and feeds on its blood.

Parasitoid
A parasite that develops inside or on its host but eventually kills it is called a **parasitoid.** Most parasitoids are wasps or flies. This wasp is laying an egg inside a developing fly. The young wasp will feed inside the fly and kill it.

Host
An animal or plant attacked by a parasite or parasitoid is called a **host.** Even people can be hosts for parasites. There may be lice living on the skin, blood may be sucked out by mosquitoes, and tapeworms may live in the gut.

◀ A tiny **trypanosome** wriggles between human red blood cells. Discover the strange and deadly microkillers on **pages 6–13.**

◀ Tapeworms drive these flour beetles crazy. Explore the world of mind-bending parasites on **pages 22–29.**

▼ A parasitic wasp drills through soil to sting a host. Learn about insect killers on **pages 14–21.**

5

In **this** book...

...you will learn about parasites that kill or badly damage the host—the world of the killers. In chapter one, find out how tiny killers such as **bacteria** cause terrible diseases. Many use other animals, such as bloodsucking mosquitoes, to get around.

Chapter two looks at killer insects called parasitoids. These animals attack an enormous range of hosts, from tiny book lice to wriggling caterpillars and enormous spiders. Parasitoids feast on the blood and internal organs of their victims before killing them. In the final chapter, you will discover how some parasites alter the way their hosts live and act, looking at ten-legged frogs, suicidal snails, and fearsome flukes along the way.

Micro**KILLERS**

Every type of animal is attacked by parasites. Most parasites are tiny and too small to see. Yet they can cause terrible damage or even death. They infect their hosts in a variety of ways. Many use bloodsucking insects to carry them around. Some of the world's deadliest diseases are caused by these tiny terrors.

6

Human history is peppered with outbreaks of disease caused by tiny, single-celled creatures called **bacteria** and **protists.** Many of these disease-causing **organisms** are carried from animals to people or between human victims by animals that drink blood. These include mosquitoes, ticks, fleas, and lice. Despite hundreds of years of medical research, disease organisms still kill millions of people around the world every year.

Deadly plague

Bubonic plague is a lethal disease that can cause a quick and painful death. The disease is named for the painful swellings, or buboes, that form under the armpits and around the neck.

Plague is caused by a type of bacteria. The bacteria live inside the digestive systems of fleas that live on rats. The bacteria divide and their numbers increase, forming a plug that blocks the flea's gut. As the flea tries to feed on the blood of its rat **host,** blood washes back from the plug.

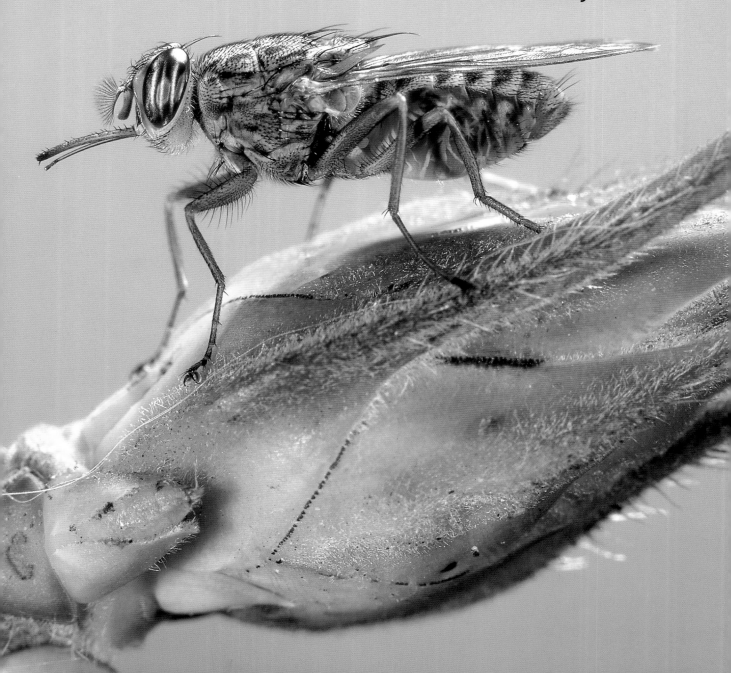

▼ *You can see some blood from the last meal of this tsetse fly inside its body.*

This blood sweeps some of the bacteria into the rat. Once infected, the rat soon dies.

As the rat population crashes due to the disease, the hungry fleas look for other sources of food. In the rat-infested homes of **medieval** Europe, the fleas often bit people. The bacteria passed into the body, and the disease quickly took hold.

Without treatment, bubonic plague kills about 75 percent of its victims. However, another disease caused by the same bacteria, pneumonic plague, is even worse. The **parasites** spread in droplets of a person's breath and kill up to 90 percent of

8

▲ *This is a rat flea. It uses its long, powerful back legs to jump on to hosts.*

▼ *A black rat. Bubonic plague was spread by fleas that lived on rats like this one.*

► *This body louse uses its strong claws to cling to body hairs. Lice like this spread the disease typhus.*

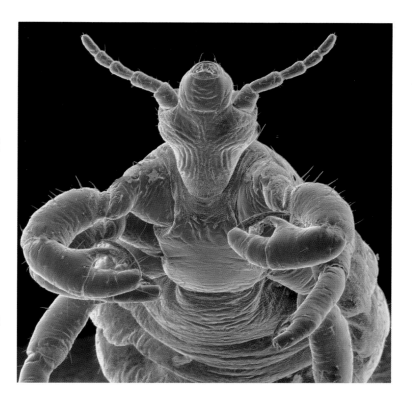

untreated people. Although both forms of plague are under control today, outbreaks still sometimes occur in parts of Africa and Asia.

A lousy disease

Like fleas, lice live on the bodies of their hosts and drink their blood. Human body lice can transmit tiny single-celled organisms called rickettsias when they feed. The rickettsias cause a deadly disease called typhus. People with typhus suffer from

Death on a massive scale

Before the 1800s, Europe had been ravaged by **epidemics** (major outbreaks) of plague for hundreds of years. The best-known of these epidemics took place during the mid-1300s. The disease moved westward from Asia along trade routes. In October 1347, merchants unwittingly brought infected black rats to Italy. The plague soon took hold, infecting and killing people with frightening speed—medieval

medicine had nothing to cope with the disease. By August 1348 the plague had spread through Europe and reached England, where it was dubbed "The Black Death" because of the black spots that appeared on victims' bodies. Some 25 million Europeans died in the epidemic—about one-third of Europe's entire population at that time.

◄ *Physicians wore masks filled with herbs to try to keep plague at bay.*

Terrible ticks

Insects are not the only animals that carry infectious diseases between hosts. Ticks are tiny relatives of spiders that pass several dangerous diseases to people. Ticks feast on blood, passing on parasites as they feed. Lyme disease, for example, is caused by bacteria that invade a person's body through the bites of infected deer ticks. Victims suffer from rashes and painful joints, but the disease is rarely fatal. However, another tick-borne disease common in the United States, Rocky Mountain spotted fever, is a noted killer. Like typhus, a rickettsia causes this disease. The parasites pass from dog tick saliva into mammals, including people. The rickettsias can cause severe damage to the nervous system, kidneys, and lungs.

◀ *A hungry dog tick waits for its next meal of blood.*

severe muscular pain and a rash that covers most of the body. Body lice pass between people in clothing and bedding, helping the disease spread. Lice thrive in crowded, unhygienic conditions, and typhus often breaks out at times of war or in refugee camps.

Flying death

Many other bloodsucking insects transmit deadly diseases. Mosquitoes, for example, spread diseases such as malaria. Malaria is caused by parasitic protists called *Plasmodium*. When a female mosquito feeds on an infected person, it draws in blood containing some of the parasites. These multiply in the mosquito's gut before moving to the **salivary glands.** The parasites are injected into another person along with the mosquito's saliva the next time the insect feeds. The parasites move through the blood to the liver, where they increase their numbers. The parasites then burst back into the blood, where they infect and

▼ *Most mosquitoes lay their eggs in murky waters, such as this slow-moving river.*

mouthparts

▼ *The life cycle of* Plasmodium, *the parasite that causes malaria.*

liver

2. The parasites invade cells in the liver, where they multiply before bursting free into the blood.

1. A mosquito bites a person, injecting saliva containing *Plasmodium* when it feeds.

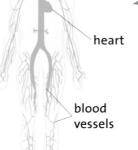

heart

blood vessels

3. The *Plasmodium* move through the blood, infecting and destroying red blood cells. Some of the parasites are taken up by a feeding mosquito.

destroy **red blood cells.** Malaria is one of the world's worst killer diseases. *Plasmodium* may kill up to 2 million people each year.

Tsetse torment

Another blood-drinking fly that spreads disease is the tsetse fly. Tsetses attack a wide range of animals. They feed on people and other mammals, as well as birds, and reptiles such as crocodiles. The flies even attack frogs and lungfish. As they feed, tsetse flies can transmit tiny parasitic protists called **trypanosomes**. One type of trypanosome lives in animals such as cows as well as people. The parasites invade a person's brain, causing a disease called sleeping sickness—one of its symptoms is uncontrollable drowsiness. Without treatment, sleeping sickness kills its victims within six months.

11

Trypanosomes cause many other diseases. The trypanosomes that cause the disease leishmaniasis, for example, live inside animals such as foxes and dogs. Sand flies that feed on the blood of an infected dog pass the trypanosomes on to people. Leishmaniasis causes fatal damage to the liver and spleen. The parasites may hide inside the body for years before signs of this terrible disease become apparent.

The kiss of death

Rather than using flies, some trypanosomes pass from person to person inside bloodsucking kissing bugs. Kissing bugs bite

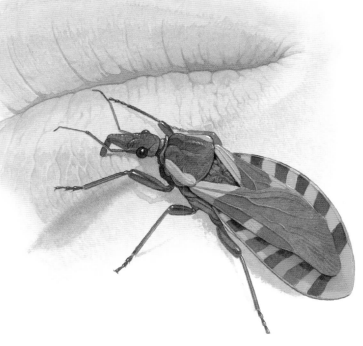

▼ *A kissing bug bites a sleeping child. Deadly trypanosomes lurk in the feces of the insect.*

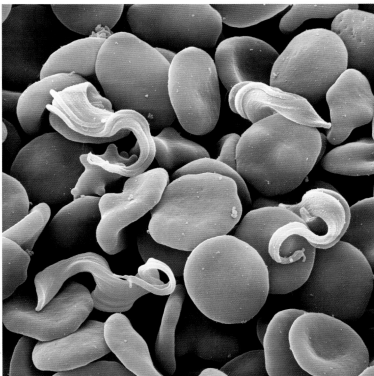

people on the face while they are asleep. As a bug feeds on blood from the bite, it defecates on its victim's skin. In the morning the parasites move into the body when the victim scratches the itchy bite. The scratching rubs the feces, which are full of trypanosomes, into the wound.

The deadly trypanosomes move through the body to attack the heart and nervous system. They cause Chagas' disease. About 50,000 people die from Chagas' disease each year in South and Central America.

◀ *Deadly trypanosomes (green) swim through a sea of human red blood cells.*

▲ *This beast is called a black fly. Female black flies feed on blood and transmit tiny worms that cause blindness in people.*

Biting black flies

Not all tiny parasites are lethal. Some do not kill their victims but still cause terrible damage. Black flies transmit little worms as they drink human blood. The worms live inside the person's body, and a buildup of dead worms in the eyes causes blindness. This is called river blindness because the flies live near rivers and swamps.

KEY FACTS

■ A range of deadly human diseases are caused by tiny creatures such as protists and bacteria.

■ Many disease-causing organisms travel from host to host inside insects or ticks.

■ Most insects that transmit diseases, including mosquitoes, fleas, and lice, are blood drinkers.

■ In the past, outbreaks of disease caused by bacteria killed millions of people.

■ Up to 2 million people are killed each year by the world's worst killer disease, malaria.

The Weird World of **PARASITOIDS**

Parasitic wasps and flies have some of the most bizarre life cycles in the animal kingdom. They inject their eggs into other animals, or the young burrow their own way in. Once inside, the larvae munch through the internal organs of their still-living host. The larvae may also release lethal chemicals, but either way the host is killed.

People often think of wasps as black-and-yellow insects that live together in nests and annoy us on summer days. Yet most wasps are different. They are called parasitic wasps. These wasps live alone and use long, rigid egg tubes to pierce the skins of other insects and lay eggs inside them. The tubes can drill deep into wood or soil to reach hidden **hosts.**

Parasitic wasp **larvae** (young) develop inside or on the surface of the host. The larvae feed on the host's organs or body fluids. The wasps kill their host when they are ready to **pupate** (become adult). Killers like these are called **parasitoids.**

Not all parasitoids are wasps, though. Many parasitic flies also kill their hosts as they develop. There are even a few types of

▼ *Parasitic wasp larvae have spun cocoons on the body of their host, a moth caterpillar.*

parasitoid beetles. Some beetle larvae wriggle into fly **pupae** (larvae changing into adults). They munch through the fly's body before pupating inside its **cocoon.**

Finding a host

Adult parasitoids must get an egg or larva into close contact with a host. Some parasitic flies lay their eggs on leaves. Caterpillars eat the leaves and swallow the eggs. The eggs then hatch inside the caterpillars.

Most adult parasitoids, however, track down hosts for their young. Some parasitoids are guided by plants. Pine trees release chemicals from their leaves when they are attacked by beetles. These chemicals alert parasitic wasps that home in on the beetles. Some hosts give themselves away. Meal moth wasps, for example, detect chemicals in the saliva of feeding

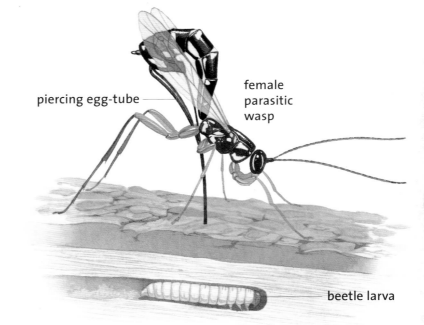

piercing egg-tube

female parasitic wasp

beetle larva

caterpillars. Some parasitic flies can even home in on the songs their mole cricket hosts sing when trying to attract mates to their underground burrows.

A chemical world

Along with the egg, parasitic wasps inject a chemical cocktail into the host. The chemicals **paralyze** the host, making it unable to move. They also alter host tissues, making them more

▲ *The larvae of many beetles live in tunnels they dig in wood. Parasitic wasps attack the beetles by drilling down through the bark with their egg tubes.*

▶ *When caterpillars eat cabbage leaves, the plants release chemicals into the air. Parasitic wasps follow the chemical trail, then lay their eggs inside the caterpillars.*

16

◀ Prickly, poison-tipped hairs do not stop a parasitic wasp from injecting an egg inside this caterpillar.

tasty for the growing larva. Some wasps paralyze their hosts only briefly. They usually attack young hosts that soon recover and continue to develop. Other wasps paralyze their victims for good; their larvae must feed as fast as they can before the host dies. These wasps usually attack adult hosts.

When ready to pupate, both types of parasitic wasps kill their hosts by munching important organs or by releasing lethal chemicals into their bodies.

Getting crowded

Parasitic wasps usually lay just one egg in each victim, but a single caterpillar or aphid can contain many young wasps. Sometimes these all come from a single egg that divides again and again to produce a lot of hungry larvae. Hundreds of adult wasps can emerge from a single host. For most parasitoids, however,

17

The tiniest of insects

Parasitoids that attack the eggs of other insects can be incredibly tiny. The smallest insect known to science is a type of fairy wasp. Discovered in 1997, this tiny wasp measures just 0.14 mm long—smaller than the period at the end of this sentence. These insects are parasitoids of book louse eggs. Each book louse egg can contain up to three male and one female fairy wasp. The males are blind and wingless, and serve only to mate. They attach to females with their legs as they emerge together from the book louse egg. The female wasps are larger than the males and have eyes and wings. After mating, the females fly away to find other book louse eggs.

18

the presence of other larvae inside the host spells trouble. For example, two types of parasitic wasps lay their eggs inside the green clover worm. This caterpillar defends itself by jumping off the leaf it is feeding on. It then dangles out of reach on a silken thread. However, one parasitic wasp can climb down the thread. It temporarily paralyzes the caterpillar and lays an egg inside.

Before the clover worm recovers and carries on feeding, it may attract the attention of another type of wasp. This second wasp hauls the defenseless caterpillar back to the leaf and lays another egg in its body. The young of this second wasp feeds on and kills the young of the first wasp. The clover worm, however, is still doomed to die. A parasitoid that eats another parasitoid inside a host is called a **hyperparasitoid.**

▲ *An adult parasitic fly eats flower nectar, unlike its insect-eating young.*

◀ *This caterpillar has been attacked by a parasitic fly. The cluster of eggs near its head will soon hatch, and the fly larvae will burrow inside to feed.*

▶ *These wasps are injecting their eggs into fruit fly eggs.*

Ladykillers

Ladybugs are fierce **predators** of aphids and other bugs, but they have deadly enemies of their own. They are stalked by a type of parasitic wasp. The wasp thrusts its egg tube into a ladybug's body and lays a single egg inside the beetle. When the egg hatches, the larva kills off any other parasitoid eggs and larvae before settling down to feed. When it is ready to become adult, the young wasp bites through the nerves that control the ladybug's legs. The wasp then breaks out of the host's body and spins a cocoon between its legs. The ladybug is still alive but cannot move. Its bright colors warn other animals that it tastes bad, and it can release foul-tasting chemicals from joints in its legs when threatened. These defenses now protect the pupating parasitic wasp. Eventually the wasp becomes an adult and flies away. The paralyzed host is left to starve.

ladybug

wasp pupa

▲ *A wasp's cocoon rests beneath a paralyzed ladybug.*

19

Foes of deadly spiders

With their insect-trapping webs and dangerous **venom** (poison), spiders might seem like powerful enemies of wasps. Some parasitic wasps, however, attack spiders, paralyzing them and making them hosts for their larvae.

Even the mightiest of spiders are under threat. Large tarantulas and wolf spiders, for example, are attacked by the hawk wasp, a huge insect that measures up to 4 inches (1 cm) long. Most spiders have no defense against parasitic wasps. Some burrowing spiders flee their homes in panic, while others simply freeze in terror. Some wasps use the spider

◀ A spider wasp digs a chamber for its catch, a wheel spider. The wasp will lay an egg on the spider's body before sealing the tomb.

burrow as a nest. They drag the paralyzed spider to part of the burrow where the temperature is just right for the growing larva. Then they seal the entrance.

Web-dwelling spiders are also at risk from wasps. Mud-dauber wasps pluck spiders from their webs and sting them on the ground. These wasps build their own nests with blobs of mud.

They pack the nest with paralyzed spiders that become food for the young wasps.

Ichneumon wasps do not drag away web spiders. Instead, an ichneumon wasp stings a spider on the web and lays an egg on its body. It then leaves the spider to recover with the wasp's egg safely attached. Some web spiders escape from wasp attack

▼ Mud-dauber wasps pack their nests with paralyzed spiders. These form a living food supply for the wasp larvae.

mud-dauber wasp larva

by abandoning their webs and leaping to the ground. One species of wasp exploits this. The wasp is a parasitoid of labyrinth spiders, which live on webs in small groups. The wasp zooms low over the spiders' web, sending them diving for cover. The wasp watches the fall of the larger spiders, which would make the best homes for her young. She swoops down and stings them on the ground before they can escape.

Off with her head

Some ants suffer what may be the most gruesome death in the insect world. Tiny flies often hover above trails of ants. When a fly has chosen a victim, it darts down and quickly lays an egg inside the ant's body. The ant is stunned but soon returns to work. The fly larva munches through the ant's body until it reaches the head. There it feeds on the ant's brain. When the fly is ready to pupate, it releases chemicals that destroy the tissue connecting the ant's head to the rest of its body. The ant's head drops off, giving the fly a safe place to pupate. These terrible parasitoids are called ant-decapitating flies—*decapitate* means "to chop off someone's head!"

KEY FACTS

- Most parasitoids are either wasps or flies.
- Some parasitoids live inside the body of the host. Others remain attached to the outside of the host's body.
- The hosts of parasitoids are killed.
- Even the largest spiders are attacked by parasitoids.
- Farmers use parasitoids to attack crop pests.

▲ This fire ant has lost its head. The head capsule provides a safe hideout for an ant-decapitating fly larva. The larva changes into an adult inside it.

Helpful parasitoids

Although ant-decapitating flies are lethal to ants, they may be helpful to people. When these flies are around, ants spend much less time foraging for food, and the colony declines.

Scientists are looking for ways to use the flies to control fire ants. When threatened, fire ants attack people and other animals in large numbers and give very painful bites.

Farmers use parasitoids to help control many other pests, especially insects that feed on crop plants. For example, the stem-borer moth, a pest of sugar cane throughout warmer parts of the world, has been successfully controlled by two parasitoids. One is a killer wasp, the other is a deadly fly.

21

Controlling
BODY and **MIND**

22

Once inside the body, many parasites take control of the way their host lives and acts. The parasites may destroy organs, make the host grow new body parts, and even release mind-bending chemicals as they take over. Hosts, however, are not without defenses and have some tricks of their own to help defeat their parasitic enemies.

Parasites can have devastating effects on the bodies of their **hosts.** Some live and develop in the **sex organs,** damaging them in the process. For the host, this is disastrous since it becomes **sterile** (unable to produce young). The parasite benefits, though. Without the distraction of breeding, the host lives longer and devotes more of its time and energy to feeding. This provides more resources for the parasite.

Create and destroy

There are many different types of sex organ parasites. Some types of nematode worms, for example, grow in the sex organs of houseflies. This makes the flies sterile. Houseflies can spread diseases such as cholera. So people use these little worms to help control

▼ *A parasitic* Sacculina *barnacle bulges from underneath the body of a shore crab.*

force their hosts to grow a tube called a respiratory funnel. This is an envelope of tissue that surrounds the larva and plugs into the **spiracles** (air holes) of the host. The fly larva breathes through the funnel.

One of the most dramatic disruptions of host growth is caused by a type of flatworm. The worms burrow into the growing limb buds of tadpoles. This completely changes the way the limbs develop. When the tadpoles become froglets, they may have as many as ten legs! These multilegged frogs are unable to swim well and are easy prey for herons. The flatworms then live inside the bird's body.

24

▲ Houseflies can spread diseases such as cholera. The bacteria that cause cholera infect the human gut and cause vomiting and diarrhea. People can die within just a few days of infection.

the flies, which cannot breed once infected. Worms called schistosomes drill into the bodies of freshwater snails and stop them from producing or laying eggs. After leaving the snail, the parasites search for people bathing in the water. The schistosomes burrow inside to complete their life cycle, causing a disease called bilharzia.

Some parasites are able to make the host grow new body parts. Tachinid fly **larvae**

Beastly barnacles

Most adult barnacles live secured to underwater rocks, but *Sacculina* barnacles are very different. Young female *Sacculina* float through the ocean, but rather than settling on a rock they land on the limb of a crab. A female *Sacculina* inches up to a joint in the crab's tough outer casing. Most of the female's body is discarded, apart from a

▶ Two tiny schistosomes. The female lives within a groove on the underside of the larger male worm.

female

male

Healthy hosts

Although hosts lose lots of nutrients to their parasites, they do not always end up small and sickly. Infection with parasites sometimes leads to an increase in size. This is called gigantism. Sticklebacks infected with tapeworms, for example, grow more quickly and keep in better shape than uninfected fish. Parasitized sticklebacks live longer and are better equipped to survive

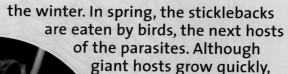

the winter. In spring, the sticklebacks are eaten by birds, the next hosts of the parasites. Although giant hosts grow quickly, they do not always eat more food. For example, tapeworms that infect mice release chemicals into their bodies. These make the mice better at converting food into body tissue.

◄ *Parasite attack can be good for sticklebacks.*

---

tiny blob of cells that is injected into the crab. The blob grows to form a threadlike network through the crab's body. The parasite drills a hole in the crab's skin. A male *Sacculina* injects cells through the hole. These fuse with the female inside, which begins to produce eggs. This spells disaster for the crab, as the newly fertilized female barnacle takes control.

Activities that might divert the crab from providing resources for the barnacle are brought to a halt. The crab is prevented from shedding its skin, so it cannot grow. The barnacle destroys the crab's sex organs, so it cannot mate. When the young *Sacculina* are ready to swim away, the female makes the crab squeeze them out through the little hole.

Mysterious mind control

Many **parasitoids** control the behavior of their hosts. Thick-headed fly larvae live inside bees. When the larva of one species is ready to become adult, it forces its host, a bumblebee, to drop to the ground. The bee then digs a burrow in the soil and crawls

▲ *A leopard frog that was infected by flatworms when it was a tadpole is an easy catch for a heron.*

Driving spiders crazy

One type of orb-weaver spider is attacked on its web by an unusual parasitic wasp. The wasp lays an egg on the spider's body. The spider soon recovers, but the larva drills into the orb-weaver and begins to feed on the tasty fluids inside. When the wasp is ready to pupate, it injects fast-acting chemicals into the spider that make it spin a very different type of web. This forms a sturdy scaffold that hangs down from the orb web. When the spider's work is done, the larva injects another chemical that kills the spider. The wasp feasts on the corpse. It then spins a **cocoon** inside the silken scaffold to pupate.

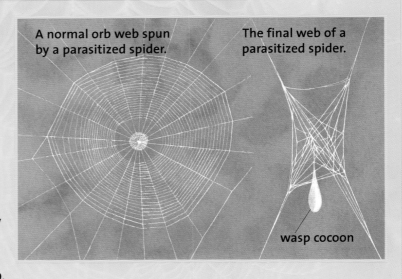

A normal orb web spun by a parasitized spider.

The final web of a parasitized spider.

wasp cocoon

▲ *The webs of a parasitized orb-weaver spider.*

inside. There it is killed by the fly larva. The larva then **pupates** in the safety of the burrow. *Aphidius* wasps also direct their hosts to safe places. The wasps' larvae live inside aphids. In fall, the larvae make the aphids move to cracks

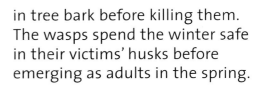

▼ *If attacked by parasitic worms, this Gammarus may become easy prey for fish.*

in tree bark before killing them. The wasps spend the winter safe in their victims' husks before emerging as adults in the spring.

An invitation to lunch

The master mind-benders in the animal kingdom, however, are parasitic worms and wormlike flukes. Many of these have more than one host—one is usually a **predator** of the other, and the parasites spend part of their life cycle in each. One of the hosts is forced to commit suicide on the parasite's behalf. The parasites alter the behavior of the host, increasing the chances of it being caught and eaten by a predator. Some thorny-headed worms, for example, attack tiny underwater animals called *Gammarus*. The worms force *Gammarus* to swim toward the surface, where they are caught by sticklebacks, the parasites' next hosts. The worms even use a lure to attract the fish. The bright orange bodies of the parasites glow through the skin of *Gammarus*.

Voodoo flukes

The life cycles of behavior-altering flukes can be very complex. The eggs of lancet flukes are swallowed by a snail. The eggs hatch inside the snail, and the flukes quickly reproduce. The snail gets rid of the parasites by coating them in balls of slime that are dumped on the ground. Ants find these slime balls very tasty and swallow them. The flukes wriggle through the ant's body toward its head. The parasites then affect the ant's brain. During a cool evening, the flukes force the infected ant to

▶ *The mind of this bewildered ant has been taken over by flukes. They have forced it to climb a blade of grass and clamp on tight with its mouthparts.*

27

▼ *Grazing cattle, as well as snails and ants, are hosts for parasitic lancet flukes.*

clamber up a long grass stalk. They then make it clamp its mouthparts securely to the stem. The ant remains under the flukes' spell, unable to move, until it is accidentally eaten by a grazing cow. The flukes then live inside

Far-reaching importance

Parasites that take control of their host's behavior are very common. Many different creatures in one area can be affected by a range of parasites. This helps control the numbers of the animals that live there. For example, flour beetles infected with rat tapeworms are slow to hide when threatened with danger. They are easy prey for the next host of the parasites, a rat. So, the tapeworms help regulate the numbers of beetles.

The way the rat acts may also be altered by parasites. **Protists** called *Toxoplasma* live in the brains of rats. An infected rat loses its usual cautiousness and wanders around outdoors in the daytime. It is soon caught and eaten by a cat. The *Toxoplasma* parasites complete their life cycle inside the cat's stomach. In this case, the parasites help control the numbers of rats.

the liver of the cow, releasing eggs into the cow's feces. If the ant has not been swallowed by sunrise, the flukes release their grip. The ant then wanders off to rejoin its nestmates until the next evening, when the persistent parasites try again.

Tempting tentacles

Another snail-attacking fluke goes to extreme lengths to dupe its next host, a small bird. The fluke forces the snail to move around in the daytime. The parasite extends a series of branches into the snail's tentacles. The branches pulse with yellow, orange, and black bands of color that attract birds. The branches also make the snail's tentacles wriggle like tasty worms. A bird that pecks off and eats the tentacles then becomes the fluke's next host.

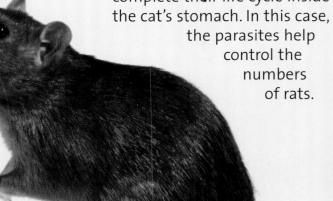

▲▼ *A brown rat (below) with parasites living inside its brain provides an easy snack for a hungry cat (above).*

28

Fighting back

Hosts are not without a few tricks of their own in the war against parasitoids. A worker bee with a young, growing wasp larva feeding inside it begins to look for food at night as well as day. Lower nighttime temperatures slow the development of the parasitoid. The colony as a whole benefits because extra food is brought in by the infected bees.

In contrast, a rise in body temperature is used by many animals to fight smaller invaders, such as fungi and **bacteria.** The temperature of an insect's body depends on how warm its surroundings are. To warm up, an insect moves to a hotter spot or basks in the sun for a while with its wings outstretched. Mammals and birds are able to produce their own body heat, and they can raise their temperature in times of infection.

Both insects and people have cells in their blood that destroy invading parasites. A rise in body temperature helps these cells work more efficiently.

▲ *A parasitic wasp larva lives inside this worker honeybee. The bee forages for food at night to slow the parasitoid's growth.*

KEY FACTS

■ Many parasites are able to take control of the minds and bodies of their hosts.

■ Parasites may destroy parts of the host or make it grow new tissues that help the parasites survive.

■ Many parasites force their hosts to allow themselves to be easily caught and eaten by other animals.

■ Hosts fight invaders with changes in body temperature.

Things to Do

Pet parasitoids

Most colonies of aphids and caterpillars contain some insects infected by **parasitoids.** But the best way to be sure of seeing parasitic wasps is by keeping some galls.

Gall-forming wasps inject their eggs into growing twigs. The growth of the twig is altered to form a gall. This is a lump of plant tissue inside which the developing wasp

◀ *These may look like acorns but they are oak apples. Each contains a growing gall wasp larva and perhaps many more young wasps.*

larva feeds, safe from **predators.**

Oak trees are a great place to look. Their galls are called oak apples. Near the end of summer, pick an oak twig that bears galls. Set the broken end of the twig into a bottle filled with water. Then cover the leaves with a clear plastic bag secured with an elastic band. Leave the leav for a week or so, then check inside the bag. You will be amazed to see the wasps that have emerged. As well as a gall-forming wasp, there may b others that steal food by nibbli at the gall. All these wasps ma host many **hyperparasitoids**— to 17 different types of wasps may live inside a single gall!

Books and websites

■ Downer, John. *Weird Nature*. Toronto: Firefly Books, 2002.

■ Knutson, Roger. *Fearsome Fauna*. New York: W. H. Freeman, 1999.

■ *The Wonderful World of Insects* http://www.earthlife.net/insects/six.html

■ *Loads of insect fun at* http://www.insectlore.com

Words to Know

bacteria
Very small single-celled organisms

cocoon
Silken case spun by many pupating insects

epidemic
Widespread outbreak of a disease

host
Animal or plant that supports a parasite

hyperparasitoid
Parasitoid that feeds on and kills another parasitoid inside the same host

larva
Young of an insect such as a fly (plural: larvae)

medieval
Period of European history between around 800 C.E. and 1500 C.E.

organism
Any type of living thing, including plants, animals, bacteria, and protists

paralyze
To make something unable to move

parasite
Any organism that benefits at the expense of another

parasitoid
Parasite that kills its host

predator
Animal that eats other animals

protist
Animal- or plantlike single-celled organism

pupa
Insect life stage in which adult structures, such as wings, form (plural: pupae)

pupate
To change from an insect larva to an adult

red blood cell
Cell in the blood that carries oxygen around the body

salivary gland
Organ that produces saliva, a liquid that helps break down food. The saliva of some insects may contain parasites that are passed to a host when the animal feeds

sex organ
Organ that produces sperm or eggs, which fuse to produce young

spiracle
Hole in an insect's tough outer skin through which the animal breathes

sterile
Unable to produce young

symbiosis
Close relationship between different types of creatures (plural: symbioses)

trypanosome
Tiny protist that causes disease

venom
Poison injected into another animal

Index

32